PreTime® Piano

Kids' Songs

Primer Level

Beginning Reading

D1398348

Arranged by

Nancy and Randall Faber

Production Coordinator: Jon Ophoff
Design and Illustration: Terpstra Design, San Francisco
Engraving: Dovetree Productions

FABER
PIANO ADVENTURES®
3042 Creek Drive
Ann Arbor, Michigan 48108

A NOTE TO TEACHERS

PreTime® Piano Kids' Songs is a collection of songs that brings special joy to children. The simplicity, humor, and charm of the selections will enhance the enjoyment of beginning piano for students and parents alike. (After all, many of these songs have been passed down from generation to generation!)

PreTime® provides the earliest level of reading for the beginning pianist. There are no dotted rhythms and eighth notes are used only sparingly. Tasteful illustrations and use of color add to the charm of the *PreTime®* books.

PreTime® Piano Kids' Songs is part of the *PreTime® Piano* series arranged by Faber and Faber. "PreTime" designates the primer level of the *PreTime® to BigTime® Piano Supple-mentary Library. Pretime®* graduates can move directly into *PlayTime® Piano* (Level 1).

Following are the levels of the supplementary library which lead up to *BigTime®*.

PreTime® Piano	(Primer Level)
PlayTime® Piano	(Level 1)
ShowTime® Piano	(Level 2A)
ChordTime® Piano	(Level 2B)
FunTime® Piano	(Level 3A – 3B)
BigTime® Piano	(Level 4)

Each level offers books in a variety of styles, making it possible for the teacher to offer stimulating material for every student. For a complimentary detailed listing, e-mail faber@pianoadventures.com or write us at the mailing address below.

Teacher Duets

Optional teacher duets are a valuable feature of the *PreTime® Piano* series. Although the arrangements stand complete on their own, the duets provide a fullness of harmony and rhythmic vitality. And not incidentally, they offer the opportunity for parent and student to play together.

Helpful Hints

1. The student should know his part thoroughly before the teacher duet is used. Accurate rhythm is especially important.

2. Rehearsal numbers are provided to give the student and teacher starting places.

3. The teacher may wish to count softly a measure aloud before beginning, as this will help the ensemble.

ISBN 978-1-61677-032-7

TABLE OF CONTENTS

Mickey Mouse March

Hand Position

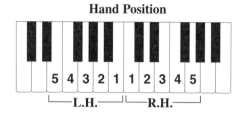

Words and Music by
JIMMIE DODD

Brightly

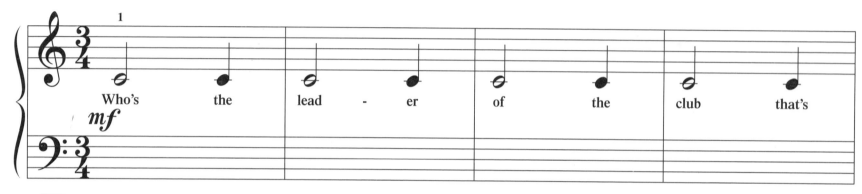

Who's   the   lead - er   of   the   club   that's

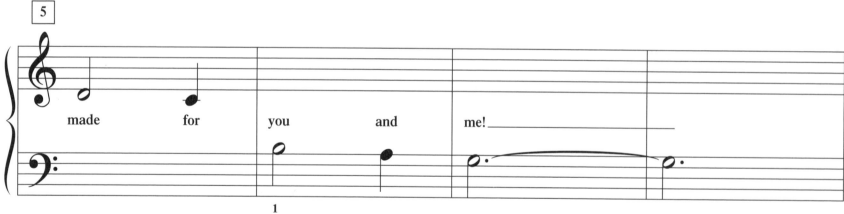

made   for   you   and   me! _____

Teacher Duet: (Student plays 1 octave higher)

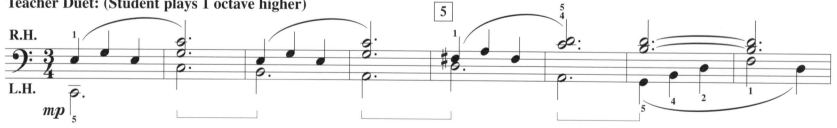

Winnie the Pooh

from Walt Disney's *Winnie the Pooh and the Honey Tree*

Words and Music by
RICHARD M. SHERMAN
and ROBERT B. SHERMAN

Hand Position

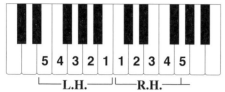

Moderately fast

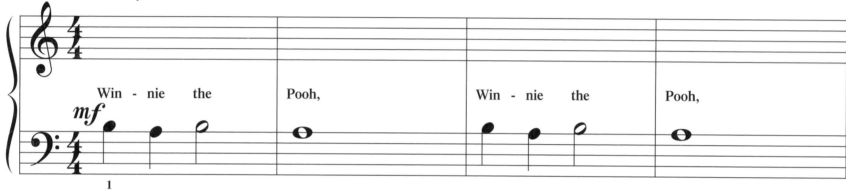

Win - nie the Pooh, Win - nie the Pooh,

tub - by lit - tle cub - by all stuffed with fluff. He's

Teacher Duet: (Student plays 1 octave higher)

R.H.

L.H.

mp

with pedal

9

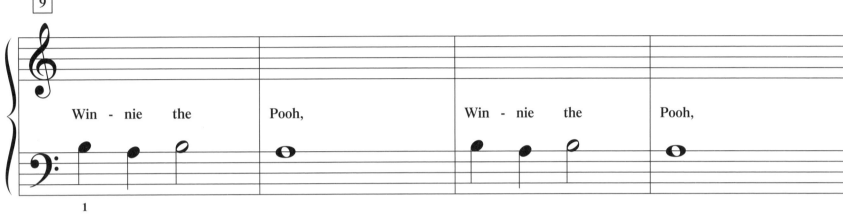

Win - nie the Pooh, Win - nie the Pooh,

13

wil - ly nil - ly sil - ly ole bear.

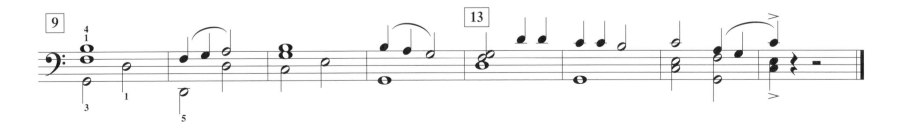

Bingo

Hand Position

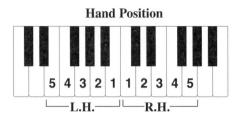

5 4 3 2 1 1 2 3 4 5

└─ L.H. ─┘ └─ R.H. ─┘

Traditional

Brightly

mf

A farm er had a big black dog, and Bin go was his name o.

5

f B I N G O, B I N G O,

Teacher Duet: (Student plays 1 octave higher)

R.H.

L.H.

mp

mf-pp

On Top of Spaghetti

Hand Position

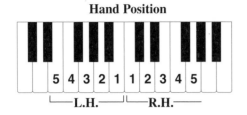

5 4 3 2 1   1 2 3 4 5

L.H.   R.H.

Moderately fast, with spirit

Words and Music by
TOM GLAZER

ones on top   Right
ones on the Bottom Left

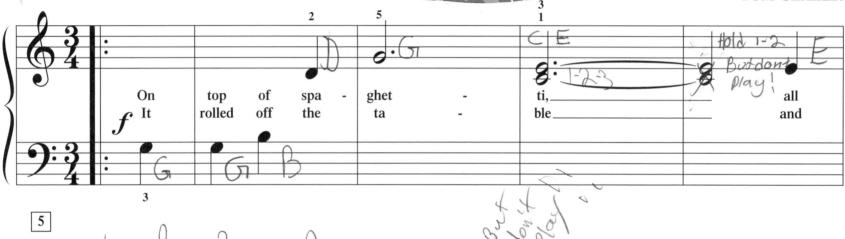

On   top   of   spa - ghet -   ti, _____   all   and
It   rolled   off   the   ta -   ble _____

Hold 1-2 But don't Play!

But don't Play it

cov - ered   with   cheese, _____   I
on - to   with   the   floor, _____   And

Teacher Duet: (Student plays 1 octave higher)

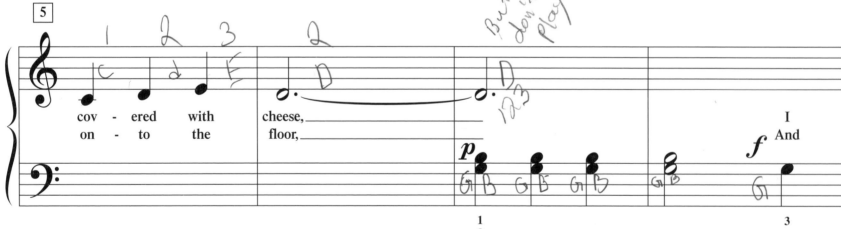

R.H.

L.H.

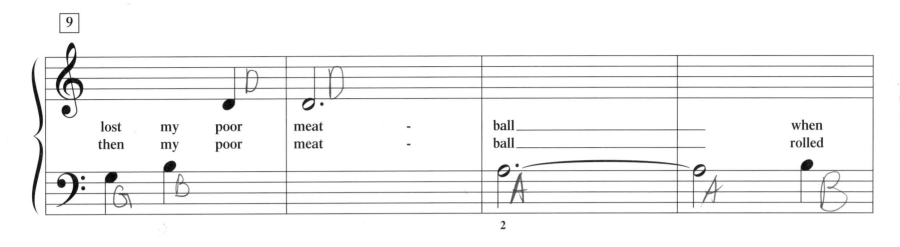

lost   my   poor   meat - ball _____   when
then   my   poor   meat - ball _____   rolled

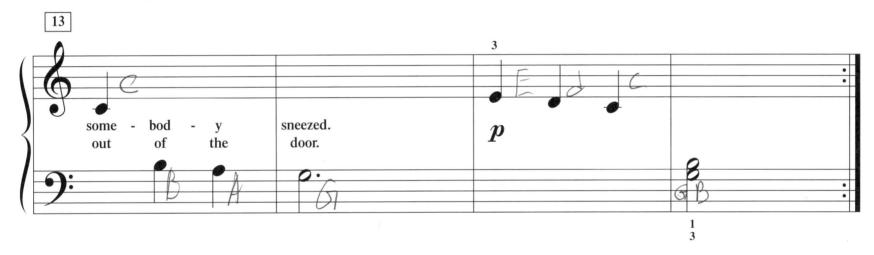

some - bod - y   sneezed.
out   of   the   door.

p

2. It rolled in the garden and under a bush,
   And then my poor meatball was nothing but mush.
   The mush was as tasty as tasty could be,
   And early next summer, it grew into a tree.

3. The tree was covered with beautiful moss;
   It grew lovely meatball and tomato sauce.
   So if you eat spaghetti all covered with cheese,
   Hold onto your meatballs and don't ever sneeze.

A-Tisket, A-Tasket

dropped   it,   I   dropped   it,   yes   on   the   way   I   dropped   it.   A

lit - tle   girl - ie   picked   it   up   and   took   it   to   the   mar - ket.

Mail Myself to You

Middle C Position

① —thumbs share Middle C

Words and Music by
WOODY GUTHRIE

Fast and sassy

mf

I'm gonna wrap my - self in pa - per, I'm gonna daub my - self with glue;

Stick some stamps on top my head, I'm gonna mail my - self to you.

Teacher Duet: (Student plays 1 octave higher)

R.H.

L.H. *mp*

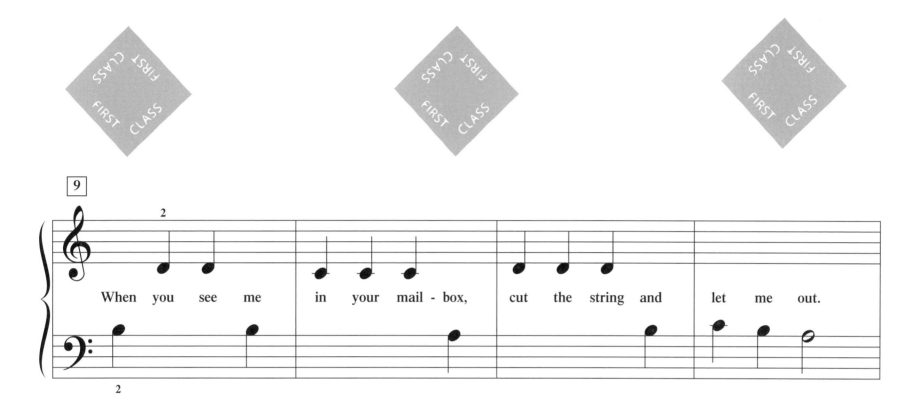

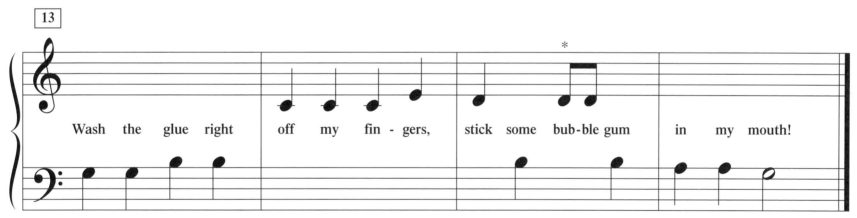

*Eighth notes may be taught by rote.

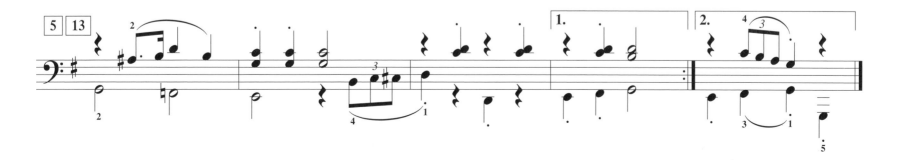

The Dwarfs' Yodel Song
(The Silly Song)

from Walt Disney's *Snow White and the Seven Dwarfs*

Words by LARRY MOREY
Music by FRANK CHURCHILL

Lively

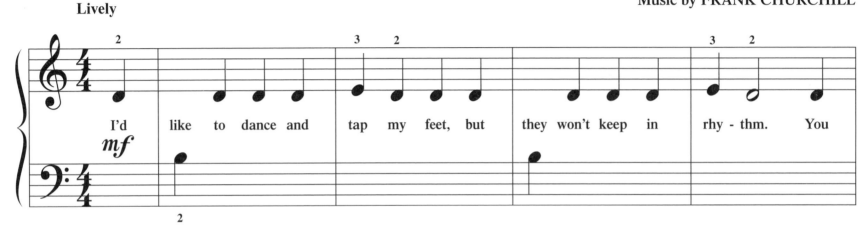

I'd like to dance and tap my feet, but they won't keep in rhy - thm. You

see, I washed them both to - day, and can't do noth - in' with 'em.

Teacher Duet: (Student plays 1 octave higher)

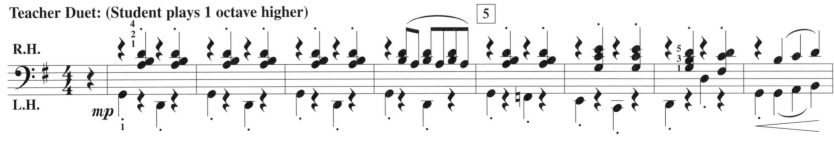

R.H.

L.H.

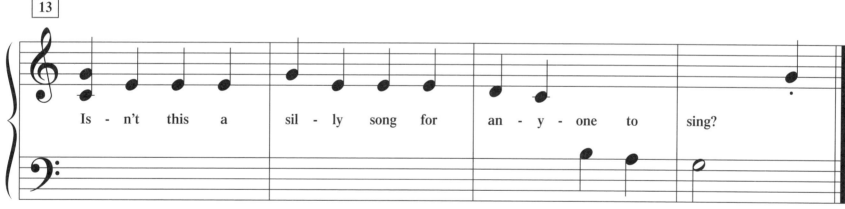

The Train Song

C 5-Finger Scale

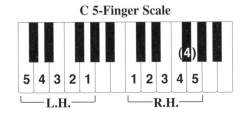

5 4 3 2 1   1 2 3 4 5
L.H.   R.H.

Traditional

With energy

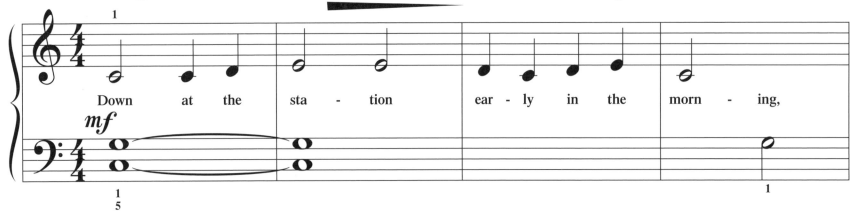

Down   at   the   sta - tion   ear - ly   in   the   morn - ing,

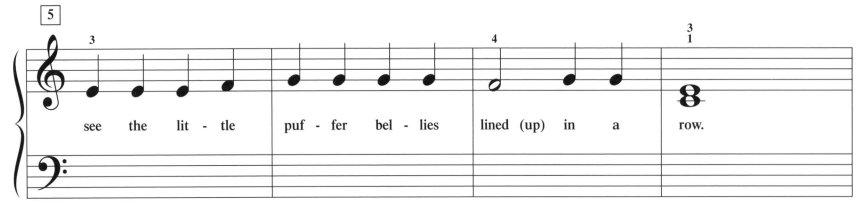

see   the   lit - tle   puf - fer   bel - lies   lined (up)   in   a   row.

Teacher Duet: (Student plays 1 octave higher)

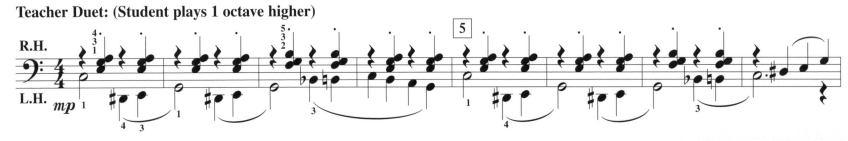

R.H.

L.H.   *mp*

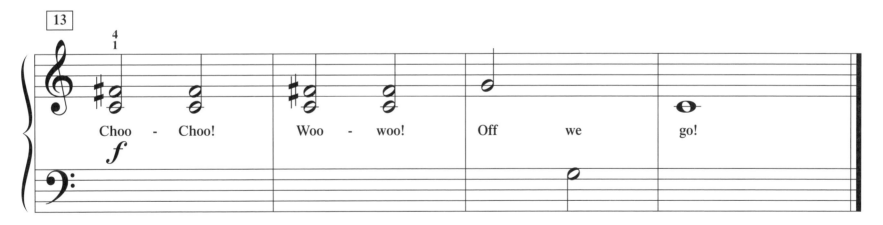

See the en - gine driv - er pull the lit - tle le - ver,

Choo - Choo! Woo - woo! Off we go!

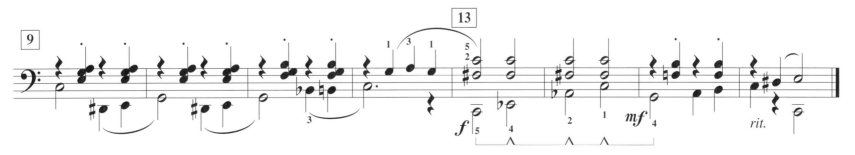

Happy Birthday to You

2-1-20

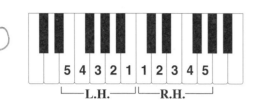

Words and Music by
MILDRED J. HILL and PATTY S. HILL

Firmly

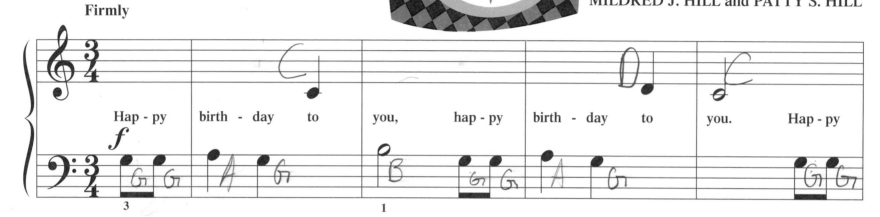

Hap - py birth - day to you, hap - py birth - day to you. Hap - py

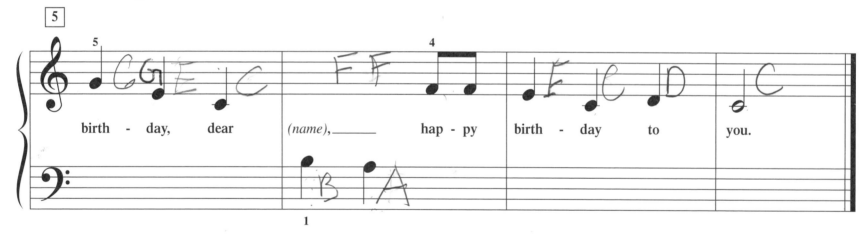

birth - day, dear (name),_____ hap - py birth - day to you.

Teacher Duet: (Student plays 1 octave higher)

R.H.

L.H.

with pedal